I0425850

BLS WORKING PAPERS

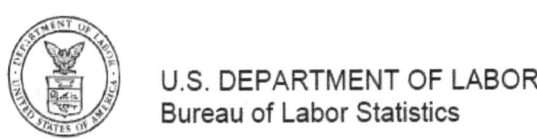

U.S. DEPARTMENT OF LABOR
Bureau of Labor Statistics

OFFICE OF COMPENSATION AND
WORKING CONDITIONS

Firm-Wide Versus Employment-Specific
Labor-Market Practices

David S. Kaplan, Instituto Tecnológico Autónomo de México
Brooks Pierce, U.S. Bureau of Labor Statistics

Working Paper 342
March 2001

This work was substantively completed while Kaplan was a research economist at the U.S. Bureau of Labor Statistics. The opinions expressed in this paper reflect the views of the authors, and do not reflect the policies of the Bureau of Labor Statistics or the views of other staff members. We gratefully acknowledge comments from seminar participants at BLS, Washington University in St. Louis, the labor studies meeting of the 2000 NBER summer institute, ITAM, and UDLA. We gratefully acknowledge financial support from the Asociación Mexicana de Cultura.

Firm-Wide Versus Establishment-Specific Labor-Market Practices[*]

January 29, 2001

David S. Kaplan
Departamento de Economía and
Centro de Investigación Económica
Instituto Tecnológico Autónomo de México
Av. Camino Santa Teresa #930
México, D.F. 10700
Mexico
E-mail: kaplan@itam.mx

Brooks Pierce
U.S. Bureau of Labor Statistics
2 Massachusetts Ave.
Room 4130
Washington, DC 20212-0001
USA
E-mail: pierce_b@bls.gov

[*] This work was substantively completed while Kaplan was a research economist at the U.S. Bureau of Labor Statistics. The opinions expressed in this paper reflect the views of the authors, and do not reflect the policies of the Bureau of Labor Statistics or the views of other staff members. We gratefully acknowledge comments from seminar participants at BLS, Washington University in St. Louis, the labor studies meeting of the 2000 NBER summer institute, ITAM, and UDLA. We also gratefully acknowledge financial support from the Asociación Mexicana de Cultura.

Abstract

Economists have devoted substantial effort to understanding why some productive activities are organized under the same firm, with the majority of empirical studies focusing on product or capital markets. Using a unique data set that links occupational data from separate establishments to the establishments' ultimate beneficial owners, we are the first to study labor markets across establishments and across industries within large and diverse firms. We use these data to determine how wages and employment in firms' different establishments and different industries are related.

We first identify patterns in the wage and occupational profiles of the industries that multi-industry firms choose to enter. We then show there to be a substantial component of wage rates common to all establishments and all industries within individual firms, even after netting out industry and occupation effects. This demonstrates the extent that internal labor markets of large, multi-establishment, multi-industry firms are linked throughout their entire organizations. Finally, we show that employment changes tend to be localized within establishments, suggesting that demand or productivity shocks to an establishment do not permeate throughout the firm.

1. Introduction

Some of the most fundamental questions in economics involve the boundaries of the firm. Although some firms are small and easy to categorize, others are diverse organizations with many establishments operating in different industries with different types of employees. We assemble a unique data set that links the labor-market information of individual establishments to their ultimate beneficial owners, in order to study the labor markets of firms with complex organizational structures.

In Table 1, we illustrate the potential for complex organizational structures within firms by providing a partial list of industries in which General Electric participates, as derived from publicly available data [Corporate Affiliations Plus (2000)].[1] As is clear from Table 1, General Electric operates in a diverse range of durable and non-durable manufacturing industries, as well as in finance and service industries. One would assume a light-bulb manufacturing plant is a very different environment from an aircraft-engine manufacturing plant, which is certainly different from a television network or a life-insurance division. Despite the apparent differences across business lines, General Electric is famous for being an integrated organization.

One reason firms like General Electric may diversify is the existence of input-market complementarities across business lines within firms; a set of inputs may be particularly productive when linked under the same firm. Skill-segregation models like Kremer (1993) are examples of such complementarities. In this class of models, high-skill employees are more productive when they are matched with other high-skill employees. To the extent that skill-

---

[1] This table was not generated using restricted-access BLS data. One should not infer that any or all of these components of GE are in our sample.

segregation models explain firm diversification, we would probably expect to see that occupational wage levels, wage changes, and employment changes would be correlated across business lines within a firm. Given the diverse nature of firms like General Electric, however, it seems natural to wonder where in the firm these skill-segregation models apply. Should these models apply across physical locations (establishments) within a firm? Should they apply across business lines (industries) within a firm?

Of course, other reasons for firm diversification exist. Firms may diversify into unrelated lines of business to smooth across sector-specific shocks to profitability [Berger and Ofek 1995], which presumably would imply no relationship in the labor markets across business lines within a firm. Firms may also diversify due to product market complementarities such as advertising or economies of scope, which has unclear consequences for labor markets across business lines. As we review in section 2, not much is known empirically about the operations of diversified firms, and almost nothing is known about their labor markets. Our goal is not to test competing theories of firm diversification. Our goal is simply to document the dimensions on which labor markets appear similar across organizational units within a firm.

In section 3, we describe our data. In section 4, we investigate the above issues by examining firms that operate in more than one industry. Such firms tend to enter either industries with high-skill occupations or industries with low-skill occupations, but tend not to enter both high-skill industries and low-skill industries. We also show that firms tend to enter only high-wage industries or only low-wage industries, even after netting out the industries' occupational distributions.

We describe in section 5 our empirical technique for analyzing wage and employment correlations after netting out industry and occupational effects. We use this technique in section

6 to look across business lines and decompose the correlations of these adjusted wage and employment measures into components that reflect establishment-specific components, industry within firm components, and firm-wide components. We find that wage changes and employment changes are not correlated across industries within a firm. However, even after controlling for fixed industry effects, occupation effects, and other covariates, we find that wage levels for all jobs throughout all business lines in a firm are correlated. That is, we estimate a common component to wages throughout a diversified firm, even when comparing different jobs in different establishments in different industries.

2. Related Literature

Much has been learned recently about the role that employers play in the labor market.[2] In particular, Abowd Kramarz and Margolis (1999) use firm-level data to show that wage differences across firms have 3 important components: differences in the observable characteristics of workers, differences in the unobservable characteristics of workers, and differences in wages after controlling for both observable and unobservable characteristics (wage policies).[3]

Abowd, Kramarz, and Margolis (1999) use the firm as the unit of analysis, implicitly relying on the wage policies across all establishments and industries within a firm being uniform. Other studies, such as Groshen (1991) and Bronars and Famulari (1997), use the establishment as the unit of analysis and must ignore the fact that multiple establishments might share a common

---

[2] See Abowd and Kramarz (1999) for a survey on the literature of matched employer-employee data.
[3] Abowd, Kramarz, and Margolis (1999) use a definition of employer that is broader than an establishment but less broad than our firm definition.

owner. In our paper, we estimate the relative importance of wage components common to entire firms and wage components that are shared by workers at more narrowly defined levels of organizational structure.

Although we are the first to disentangle the separate effects of firm and establishment affiliation, there exists some indirect evidence that wage decisions or hiring decisions are influenced both by firm-wide and establishment-specific factors. Brown and Medoff (1989) and Troske (1999) show that cross-sectional wages are positively correlated with both establishment size and firm size. These results suggest either that wage policies or hiring policies are determined by both establishment-specific and firm-wide factors. After we estimate wage correlations within and across various levels of a firm's organizational structure, we then show that only a small portion of these correlations can be modeled with establishment- and firm-size variables.

Although we are the first to study wage and employment correlations across the industries within diversified firms, other aspects of these firms have already been studied. One strand of research [Schmalensee (1985), Rumelt (1991), McGahan and Porter (1999)] examines the extent to which accounting profits are specific to industries as opposed to being specific to firms or to particular business lines within firms. This literature tends to find relatively little common profitability across different business lines within a given diversified firm.

Another strand of research focuses on the effects of internal capital markets and investment across business lines in multi-industry firms. This literature finds evidence that internal capital markets are linked across business lines. Berger and Ofek (1995) find that multi-industry firms invest more in unproductive industries than do single-industry firms. Berger and Ofek also find evidence that unproductive lines of business within a firm drain resources away

4

from more productive lines of business.[4] Along similar lines, Lamont (1997) finds firms with significant oil-extraction operations responded to an exogenous decrease in oil prices by reducing investment in unrelated lines of business.

Lastly, we contribute to the literature on job creation and destruction, as summarized in Davis and Haltiwanger (1999). This literature finds that looking at aggregate movements in employment growth masks considerable heterogeneity at the establishment level. Individual establishments die and contract when an industry is growing and individual establishments are born and expand when an industry is contracting. We extend these results by estimating considerable establishment-level heterogeneity in job growth even when restricting our analysis to establishments in the same firm and same industry. Even within a growing business line within a firm, we observe some establishments reducing their employment dramatically.

3. Data: The National Compensation Survey

The National Compensation Survey (NCS) is an establishment wage survey designed to generate a nationally representative random sample of detailed jobs within establishments (see U.S. Department of Labor, 1997). A detailed job is the most narrowly defined job level recognized by the establishment's job title classification. Our wage observations are the average hourly wages for all employees within an establishment who work in a particular detailed job. We typically observe multiple detailed jobs within an establishment.

The survey encompasses large establishments in the non-agricultural, non-Federal economy. Private households and establishments with fewer than 50 employees are out of scope

---

[4] However, Chevalier (2000) notes that many of these same patterns appear before business lines are merged into diversified firms.

for the survey. Field economists visit sampled establishments at survey initiation and obtain information on the establishment and on a sample of jobs in the establishment. Since industry coding is done at the establishment level, we often observe multiple industries within a multi-establishment firm. The survey is longitudinal, with annual survey updates conducted via mail and telephone.

Establishment information in the NCS includes establishment employment, location, industry, and employer identification number (EIN). These data elements come from the sampling frame and are verified by field economists. Job-specific information includes a census occupational classification (421 categories in our data), earnings data, and work schedule information. Earnings are defined as regular payments from the employer to the employee as compensation for straight-time hourly work, or for any salaried work performed. Earnings include incentive pay and production bonuses such as commissions and piece rates. Earnings exclude premium pay for overtime, holiday, and weekend work; shift differentials; bonuses not directly tied to production; payments by third parties such as tips or referral incentives; and payment in kind such as room and board. Scheduled hours per week are measured exclusive of overtime for hourly workers; for salaried workers actual hours typically worked are measured. Earnings are converted to a dollars per hour basis using the work schedule information. Our wage measure is the log of the average wage rate among workers in the job, deflated using the CPI-U to 1999 dollars.

For the purposes of the NCS, establishments are economic units producing goods or services, auxiliary units providing support services, or central administrative offices. Figure 1 gives a schematic relating establishment and firm definitions in our data. For private sector industries in this survey, establishments are usually at a single physical location. Employer identification numbers (EINs) on the database allow us to link different establishments that have common ownership. Establishments in the same firm, however, can have different EINs; any subsidiary firms, even if they are fully owned by the parent firm, receive separate EINs. We link EINs that are owned by the same parent firm using data from the Corporate Affiliations Plus (1998).[5] Most previous labor economics researchers have used either data with establishment identifiers (not linking establishments with common ownership) or data with firm identifiers defined using EIN (thereby not linking different EINs with common ownership).

We utilize extracts from the 1997 and 1998 NCS samples. We restrict the data to include private sector establishments only. We keep observations that can be matched across years, losing about 20% of the 1997 sample observations to attrition. We also exclude data from single-establishment firms, since we are particularly interested in characterizing the correlations of wages across establishments within the same firm.[6] This restriction results in an additional 60% decrease in our sample size. Minor exclusions include deleting observations with missing occupation codes, missing industry codes, or changing firm identifiers. Since the exclusions in total are substantial, we estimate the parameters of interest using unweighted data.[7]

Table 2 presents definitions and summary statistics for our data. After making all of the exclusions mentioned above, we have wage data from 34,792 job cells. These data come from 4,320 establishments and 1,020 firms. Observing wages from multiple establishments within a

---

[5] These are the same data used by the National Register Publishing Company to produce the annual publication "Directory of Corporate Affiliations."

[6] Excluded single establishment firms may have additional establishments that were not sampled by the NCS.

[7] Sampling within strata is done with probability proportionate to employment. Therefore unweighted data gives samples which are at least partly employment-weighted (weights adjust mainly for nonresponse and differential probabilities of selection across strata). We obtain similar results when using weights.

firm is an important advantage over previous work. The sampled employment in these job cells is about 1.3 million workers in 1997.[8]

One attractive feature of our data is that industry is coded at the establishment level, allowing us to study within-firm industry heterogeneity. We observe 457 firms operating in more than one 3-digit industry and we observe 258 firms operating in more than one major industry classification.[9] This within-firm industry heterogeneity represents another advantage over the data used in Abowd, Kramarz, and Margolis (1999) who must allocate all employees within a firm to a single industry.

The major weakness of our data compared to data used in Abowd, Kramarz, and Margolis (1999) and others is that we have little information on employees. The data follow jobs—but not individuals—longitudinally. When we observe an establishment that pays high wages we therefore cannot determine whether its employees also received high wages when employed in other firms. We also do not observe worker demographics and productivity-related characteristics such as schooling.

Since our panel is based on significant exclusions from the NCS, Table 2 also presents statistics comparing our sample to the full 1997 NCS cross section. Our multi-establishment panel is more highly unionized and has larger establishments than the 1997 NCS as a whole. Jobs in our multi-establishment panel pay about 5 percent higher wages.[10] As one might expect,

---

[8] Employment in the 1997 NCS cross-section is about 2.6 million workers. The population in scope is approximately 52 million private industry workers. Therefore the NCS cross-section samples about 5 percent of the private sector employment in scope. Our multi-establishment panel includes about half of this employment.
[9] We define nine major industry categories: mining; construction; durable manufacturing; non-durable manufacturing; transportation, communications, and utilities; wholesale trade; retail trade; finance, insurance, and real estate; and services. All of our results are robust to grouping durable and non-durable manufacturing into one major industry. Finer industry categories within these major industries are based on the first three digits of the establishment's SIC industry code, and we term these "3-digit" industries.
[10] The wage differential after controlling for occupation, industry, state, union status and payroll date is about 4.3 percent.

our multi-establishment panel has somewhat more employment in manufacturing and retail trade, and less in services, than the 1997 NCS cross-section. The occupational distributions, however, are quite similar.

4. The Selection of Industries and Occupations for Diversified Firms

Our ultimate goal is to document the extent to which labor markets within large diversified firms appear similar. One reason labor markets may appear to be similar across business lines within a firm is that the firm chooses to enter industries with similar labor-market characteristics. A firm may, for example, choose to enter industries that use high-wage occupations. A firm may also choose to enter industries with high industry effects, that is, choose to enter industries that pay high wages after controlling for the occupational distribution of the industries.

To analyze these issues, we regress log wages on industry and occupation effects, along with other covariates, using our multi-establishment panel of 34,792 jobs. We estimate:

$$y = X_i\beta_i + X_o\beta_o + Z\delta + u \tag{1}$$

where y is the average of 1997 and 1998 log wages, the X_i are 3-digit industry fixed effects, the X_o are occupation fixed effects, and the Z controls include state, time, and union effects. For now we ignore error term correlations across observations within the same firm; that issue forms the basis for much of our later analysis. Our immediate focus is on describing how similar chosen industries are within a diversified firm. We do so by assigning to each establishment its 3-digit industry effect and its industry's employment-weighted average-occupation effect, and

9

comparing those effects across the different parts of the diversified firm.[11] The industry's

average-occupation effect is a summary measure of the industry's occupational content, and it at

least partly measures the average level of skill in each industry. The interpretation of the

industry effects themselves is more controversial, but they too may partly reflect skill

differences.

We do not want our results in this section to be driven by the fact that firms typically

enter similar industries, and so we restrict the sample to the 258 firms operating in more than one

major industry. We divide each multi-industry firm into two parts: the major industry with the

most employment in our sample and the rest of the firm. We then average (weighting by

employment) the 3-digit industry effects and the industry-average occupational content measures

for both parts of the firm. A typical comparison in this section is, for example, a firm with one

business line in services and one business line in durable manufacturing. Will the business lines

tend to be in industries with similar occupational distributions (both high-skill or both low-skill

industries)? Will they tend to have similar values for their fixed industry effects? The answer to

these questions, to anticipate results, is "yes".

We first examine whether firms tend to enter industries with similar occupational

distributions. At this point, we are ignoring the wages these particular firms pay and we are

ignoring the occupational distributions these firms choose. All we are analyzing now is whether

firms choose to enter industries with, on average, similar occupational distributions. Figure 2

plots the industry-average occupational content measure from each part of a diversified firm

against the similar construct for the other part.

---

[11] Equation (1) partitions industry wage differences into components due to industry differences in occupations, industry differences in other observed factors (the Z's), and unexplained industry differences in wages. Averaging the estimated components of equation (1) over observations in the same 3-digit industry gives this partition.

As is evident from figure 2, firms have a tendency to enter industries with similar values of average occupational effects. The correlation coefficient for figure 2 is 0.44. Even across major industries, it appears as if there is a benefit of uniting industries with similar skill levels under the same firm. Perhaps these results reflect skill complementarities that cross major industry boundaries, or perhaps they reflect common technologies that are used across major industry boundaries. Other explanations are also possible. Clearly, however, a pattern exists in the types of industries diversified firms choose to enter.

Figure 3 performs a similar exercise for the fixed-industry effects. We plot the employment-weighted average of fixed-industry effects for firm's largest major industry against this same measure for the rest of the firm.[12] Figure 3 therefore examines whether firms tend to choose industries that pay similar levels after controlling for the occupational distribution of these industries. Of course, these fixed-industry effects may measure nothing more than skill levels that are observable to the firms but are unobservable to us. These fixed industry effects may also reflect pay differences due to differing contracting environments (efficiency wages for example).[13]

The picture in figure 3 looks similar to that in figure 2. After controlling for the occupational distributions within industries, firms tend either to enter high-wage industries or to enter low-wage industries, but tend not to enter high-wage and low-wage industries simultaneously. The correlation coefficient of these two series is also 0.44.[14]

_____

[12] The average of fixed effects within a major industry may come from one or many 3-digit industries.

[13] See Abowd and Kramarz (2000) for evidence that industry-wage differentials are correlated with both unobservable individual heterogeneity and with fixed firm effects (wage differences that remain after netting out individual heterogeneity).

[14] Our calculations indicate that part of this relationship is due to similarities in the wages of major industries that firms enter. Part is also due to the fact that firms entering high-wage 3-digit industries in one major industry also tend to enter the high-wage 3-digit industries in other major industries.

Taken together, figures 2 and 3 tell us that, even across major industries, firms tend to enter industries with similar labor market characteristics. We are also interested, however, with the choices firms make after they decide to enter an industry. One such choice is the occupational distribution actually chosen by the firm, which may differ from industry norms. We can easily use the estimates from equation (1) to construct summary wage measures of the occupations firms hire for, after netting out the typical occupational profile in the particular industry. Specifically, we calculate the employment-weighted average of the fixed-occupation effects for the occupations chosen by each firm within each 3-digit industry. We then subtract off the industry mean, and aggregate this value for the largest major industry in each firm and the rest of each firm. This is a measure of whether the firm uses high-wage occupations, conditional on the 3-digit industries the firm enters. As it turns out, the occupational choices of firms once industry norms are netted out are related across the firms' different major industry divisions. The correlation is positive, but the correlation coefficient is only 0.12. We view this as only weak evidence of a systematic pattern across major industries in occupational choices relative to industry norms.

We have made other calculations that support the general finding of a relationship between the industries that multi-industry firms choose to enter. For example, when these firms operate in multiple 3-digit industries within the same major industry, the 3-digit industries tend to be either high-wage or low-wage (but not both) relative to the major industry average. The general finding is important because it indicates that establishments in multi-industry firms have wage rates related along some observable dimensions, in this case industry and occupation. That raises an interesting corollary question: are wages in different establishments related, after netting out the effects of observables?

5. Restricted Maximum Likelihood (REML)

In the previous section, we analyzed the industry and occupational decisions of firms across major industries. We would now like to analyze the wage and employment correlations that exist across organizational divisions after netting out industry and occupational choice. We need an estimation strategy that allows wages across jobs within an establishment to be more highly correlated than wages across establishments but within the same firm. A particularly succinct way of summarizing these wage correlation patterns is to estimate variance components at each level in the hierarchy. If, for example, one finds a relatively large estimated variance for firms' effects on wages then it follows that wages within a firm are highly correlated: the different jobs within the firm share a common component that is on average large in absolute value.

To keep the exposition simple, we present a wage model with only two levels of hierarchy: the firm and the establishment within the firm. Our main results all account for one or two additional levels of hierarchy corresponding to 3-digit industry affiliations within firms or major-industry affiliations within firms. Extending the model we present below to one with additional levels of hierarchy is straightforward.

Consider a wage determination model of the form:

$$y_{jkt} = X_{jkt}\beta_t + \psi_{f(k)} + \psi_k + \phi_{f(k)t} + \phi_{kt} + \eta_{jk} + \upsilon_{jkt}, \qquad (2)$$

where y_{jkt} is log wage for job j in establishment k in year t, X_{jkt} are covariates, and $f(k)$ is the subscript for the firm to which the establishment belongs. As in equation (1) above, the covariates are fixed state, fixed 3-digit industry, and fixed occupation effects, union coverage and month of the wage observation (interacted with year). The fixed effects, which were previously analyzed in section 4, are treated as nuisance parameters here. We are primarily interested in estimating the variances of the error components. Since we are interested in describing wage levels as well as wage changes, we posit time-varying and permanent components of variance. Assume $\psi_{f(k)}$, ψ_k, $\phi_{f(k)t}$, ϕ_{kt}, η_{jk} and υ_{jkt} are iid normally distributed mean-zero random variables with variances of $\sigma^2_{\psi,f(k)}$, $\sigma^2_{\psi,k}$, $\sigma^2_{\phi,f(k)}$, $\sigma^2_{\phi,k}$, σ^2_{η}, and σ^2_{υ} respectively.

Given estimates for the error variances we can derive wage correlations of interest, net of the fixed controls. Define $\tilde{y}_{jkt} \equiv y_{jkt} - X_{jkt}\beta_t$, which is the difference between the log wage for the job cell and the log wage we would expect from the covariates alone. We can then express the wage correlation between any two jobs as a function of the estimated variances. According to our model of wage determination, for example, the correlation of $\tilde{y}_{jkt}$ between two jobs within the same establishment in the same time period is:

$$\rho\left[\tilde{y}_{jkt}, \tilde{y}_{j'k't'}\right] = \frac{\sigma^2_{\psi,f(k)} + \sigma^2_{\psi,k} + \sigma^2_{\phi,f(k)} + \sigma^2_{\phi,k}}{\sigma^2_{\psi,f(k)} + \sigma^2_{\psi,k} + \sigma^2_{\phi,f(k)} + \sigma^2_{\phi,k} + \sigma^2_{\eta} + \sigma^2_{\upsilon}}, \tag{3}$$

which is simply the total variance of the common components divided by the total variance of all components. Looking at the numerator for the above expression, we see that this correlation has four components. These components reflect random firm effects (permanent and time varying) and random establishment effects (permanent and time varying). The numerator does not, of course, include the random job cell components σ_η^2 and σ_υ^2 since two different jobs in the same establishment would not share common draws from the distribution of those components.

Another example may be helpful. Suppose we now consider two log wage draws coming from the same firm, but different establishments and different years. In this case, the correlation is

$$\rho\left[\tilde{y}_{jkt}, \tilde{y}_{j'k't'}\right] \;=\; \frac{\sigma_{\psi, f(k)}^2}{\sigma_{\psi, f(k)}^2 + \sigma_{\psi, k}^2 + \sigma_{\phi, f(k)}^2 + \sigma_{\phi, k}^2 + \sigma_\eta^2 + \sigma_\upsilon^2},$$

since the two observations only share a permanent random firm effect.

Computational constraints prevent us from estimating all of the parameters of equation (2) simultaneously. To obtain the time-varying components of wage correlations, we estimate the following first-difference model:

$$\Delta y_{jk} \;=\; \Delta X_{jkt}\beta_t \;+\; (\textit{random firm effects})_{f(k)} + (\textit{random establishment effects})_k +$$

$$(\textit{random job cell effects})_{jk},$$

where Δy_{jk} is the change in the log wage from 1997-1998 for job j in establishment k. The random effects capture the first-differenced temporary components. The random job within establishment effects can be viewed as the statistical residual. The variances of random firm effects, random establishment effects, and random job within establishment effects correspond to $2\sigma_{\phi, f(k)}^2$, $2\sigma_{\phi, k}^2$, and $2\sigma_\upsilon^2$ respectively.

To recover the permanent components we also estimate the model:

$$\bar{y}_{jk} = \overline{X_{jk}\beta_t} + (random\ firm\ effects)_{f(k)} + (random\ establishment\ effects)_k +$$

$$(random\ job\ cell\ effects)_{jk},$$

where $\bar{y}_{jk}$ is the average log wage for the job cell across the two years in our sample. Here the

random effects at any level of aggregation incorporate the permanent effect plus the average of

two temporary effect draws. For example, the variance of random firm effects corresponds to

$$\sigma^2_{\psi,f(k)} + \frac{\sigma^2_{\phi,f(k)}}{2}.$$

Models that include both fixed and random effects are often called mixed models. We

follow a suggestion of Groshen (1991) and estimate the above mixed models through restricted

maximum likelihood (REML). REML maximizes a vector of linear combinations of the

observations that are invariant to the fixed effects of the model. That is, REML obtains estimates

of the covariance parameters of the model without obtaining estimates of the fixed effects of the

model. REML is also robust to a relaxation of the assumption of normally distributed random

effects.[15]

The main specification issues relate to choosing which fixed effects to include and how to

represent the random effects. We are especially interested in models with as complete a

hierarchical specification as possible. In particular, effects common to different establishments

might be larger when the establishments are in similar industries than when they are in dissimilar

ones. For this reason we estimate models that have random industry-within-firm effects in

---

[15] See Searle, Casella, and McCulloch (1992) for more details. Groshen (1991) estimates anova models with varying
sets of fixed effects (first a baseline specification, then one adding establishment effects, and so forth) and compares
the R-squared statistics from the models as a variance decomposition technique.

addition to those given in equation 1. We also include random major industry within firm effects when possible, but at times this additional parameter cannot be estimated. Our main constraint, aside from computational issues, is that there is relatively limited across-industry variation within firms.

6. Empirical Results

Before turning to our main results in this section, we first try to assess the magnitudes of the firm-side components of wages and employment changes. In Table 3, we present REML models for changes in log wages between 1997-1998, the average of 1997 and 1998 log wages, and percent changes in employment.[16] We include random occupation effects, random industry effects, and random establishment effects in all three models. All three models contain fixed effects for state, union status, and month (interacted with year) of observation.

Since we do not include random firm effects or random firm within industry effects, the variance of random establishment effects captures the effects of all levels of a firm's hierarchy. We then wish to compare the importance of this composite measure of firm heterogeneity to the importance of industry and occupation effects. Before we apportion firm-level heterogeneity to various levels of a firm's hierarchy, we want to establish that the magnitudes of firm-level heterogeneity are such as to justify the exercise.

Looking first at wage changes, we see the estimated variance of the random effect for the establishment is much larger than those for occupation and industry, however a one standard

---

[16] To maintain comparability with previous work we define percent change in employment as the difference between job cell employment in 1998 and 1997 divided by the average job cell employment across the two years. This treats expansions and contractions symmetrically.

deviation change in the random establishment effect results in a modest 3% change in wages. Although modest, this 3% standard deviation of random establishment effects dwarfs the magnitudes of random occupation and random industry effects in the wage-change model. Looking at average wages, we see that the variance of random establishment effects is more than half the size of the corresponding variance for 3-digit industries. A one standard deviation increase in the random establishment effect changes wages by roughly 14%. Finally turning to employment changes, we see the random establishment effects dominate occupation and industry effects, with a one standard deviation change in the random establishment effect corresponding to a 16% increase in employment.

Another way to assess magnitudes is by comparing adjusted R-squared statistics from regressions with and without establishment fixed effects. In the wage-change model, the adjusted R^2 rises from 0.05 to 0.25 with the inclusion of fixed-establishment effects to a model with fixed effects for union status, month of observation, state, 3-digit occupation, and 3-digit industry. The same exercise results in the adjusted R^2 rising from 0.80 to 0.87 in the average-wage model and from 0.04 to 0.26 in the employment change model.

We believe the results in Table 3 and the adjusted R^2 results above show that the magnitudes of employer-level heterogeneity are large enough to warrant study. We now turn to allocating these within-establishment correlations to various levels of firm hierarchy.

A. Wages

Table 4 contains our wage decomposition for our entire multi-establishment panel. In particular, Table 4 decomposes wages into permanent and time-varying components at the establishment level, at the firm within 3-digit industry level, at the firm within major industry level, and at the firm wide level. The top panel of the table shows the REML estimations of the wage-change and average-wage models. The middle panel transforms these estimates into variance estimates of the components in equation (2), and decomposes the within-establishment and within-year correlation into each of its eight components. The bottom panel shows the wage correlations between different jobs implied by the variance components.

Looking first at the wage-change results, we see that wage changes are essentially uncorrelated outside of the establishment. The average-wage results, however, show that wage levels contain significant components at all four levels of the hierarchy. That is, wage levels are correlated across all jobs and establishments within a diversified firm, but they are more highly correlated when the job cells are more closely related in the firm's organizational structure.

Looking at the middle panel, we see that only two percent of the within establishment wage correlation comes from time-varying components, almost all of which comes from the random establishment effects. About one third of the contribution of the permanent components comes from establishment effects, with the other three components making significant contributions as well.

In the bottom panel of Table 4 we see, for both wage levels and wage changes, our estimated correlations for job cells within a firm. As should be expected, wage changes are only correlated to any significant degree when the job cells are in the same establishment, while wage levels are correlated throughout an entire firm.[17]

Table 4 shows that wage levels within firms are correlated across major industries. It is unclear whether this correlation is due to wage policies or due to unobservable productivity

---

[17] The wage level correlations in the bottom panels of tables 4-6 assume wages from the same period. Since the time-varying effects are small relative to the permanent effects, wage correlations assuming wages from different periods would be of similar magnitude.

characteristics of the employees, but the labor markets within diversified firms once again appear to be related. Firms not only choose to enter industries with similar characteristics (as shown in Figures 2-3), but adopt similar wage policies or hiring policies across industries after entry.

One common way to model firm-level heterogeneity in wage regressions is by including measures of firm or establishment size [Brown and Medoff (1989), Troske (1999)]. Economists typically view these measures as proxies for unobservable sorting or proxies for unobservable characteristics of the contracting environments. Since these are the sorts of issues in which we are interested, we do not include establishment or firm size measures as controls in Table 4. Having quantified the magnitudes of within firm wage correlations, and having apportioned them to various hierarchical levels, we now turn to the question of how well these correlations could be modeled using establishment or firm size measures.

In Table 5, we add logs of establishment employment, firm employment within the 3-digit industry, firm employment within the major industry, and total firm employment as additional controls. To the extent that these additional controls reduce the values of the estimated random effects, we can say that we have modeled the wage correlations through firm-size controls.[18] We find, however, that adding firm-size controls has only a modest effect on our results.

---

[18] Our definition of firm size is the total employment in all establishments (including those not in the NCS) in all EINs that appear in our multi-establishment panel. Our definitions of firm employment within the major industry and firm employment within the 3-digit industry are analogous. We use March employment from the 1997 and 1998 BLS master business-establishment lists to construct these measures. Our establishment employment measures come from the NCS.

Looking first at wage changes, we see that the inclusion of these fixed-employment effects has no effect on the estimated variances of the random effects, indicating that wage changes cannot be modeled with employment changes.[19]

Turning now to the average-wage model in Table 5, we see that the addition of the firm size measures substantially reduces the estimated random firm effect variance. The addition of firm size measures raises the random firm*major industry effect variance. The other random effects variance estimates are basically unchanged. If taken literally, these results imply that all of the wage correlations that we estimate across major industries within a firm can be modeled with a firm-size variable, but the other size variables have little explanatory power. However, some caution is warranted, as the data often make it difficult to distinguish the firm and the firm*major industry random effects from each other.[20]

We are also interested in the extent to which unionization drives our results. Perhaps union contracts are negotiated at the firm level, which could generate many of the correlations we observe. Unfortunately, our unionization sample is too small to estimate a model like that in Table 4. We do, however, present the results of the wage models that exclude unionized workers in Table 6.

Since the wage-change results are similar to those that included all job cells, we will focus on the average-wage models. The main difference between the wage level models in Table 6 and Table 4 is that the firm-wide random effect is estimated to be insignificant in Table 6. This indicates that, after including all of our fixed effects as controls, the wage levels of non-

---

[19] The fixed effect for the change in firm employment within the 3-digit industry is statistically significant in the wage-change model, although its impact on our results is small. The other three size variables are not statistically significant.

[20] The fixed effects for both total firm employment and establishment employment are statistically significant in the average-wage model. The fixed effects for firm employment within the major industry and firm employment within the 3-digit industry are not statistically significant.

unionized jobs may not be correlated across major industries within a firm. The coefficients on the other levels of the hierarchy are similar between Tables 6 and 4, including the coefficient that shows wage levels are correlated across 3-digit industries within the same major industry. The majority of our results do not appear to be driven by unionized jobs; the same broad patterns exist using only non-unionized jobs.[21]

B. Employment Growth

Table 7 presents a REML estimation of an employment-change model with random-establishment effects, 3-digit industry effects, and random firm effects.[22] Once again, our employment change measure is the change in job-cell employment from 1997-1998, divided by the average of 1997 and 1998 employment. Note first that employment growth at the job-cell level is uncorrelated across 3-digit industries. Note next that, although employment growth is correlated across establishments within a 3-digit industry within a firm, the estimated variance of random establishment effects dwarfs that of the random 3-digit industry within firm effects. Note lastly that the variance of the residual is easily the largest variance estimated.[23]

We interpret these results as an extension of the recent lessons in the job creation and destruction literature.[24] Davis & Haltiwanger (1990, 1992) and others have shown that churning of employment is high in both strong and weak economies. That is, significant establishment-

---

[21] Results using only white-collar jobs look similar to those in Table 6, and are available on request.

[22] Random firm*major-industry effects estimates consistently hit the boundary of zero when included in the employment change models, meaning that we cannot distinguish between the random effects within and between major industry.

[23] Establishment employment includes both jobs that were sampled by the NCS and jobs that were not sampled by the NCS.

[24] Employment-change models yielded similar results when estimated separately for union and non-union jobs, as did models estimated separately for white-collar and non-white-collar jobs.

level expansions occur when an industry is contracting overall, and significant establishment-level contractions occur when an industry is expanding overall.

Our estimates show that even when a particular business-line within a firm grows, a high percentage of individual establishments are likely to contract. That is, even when a business line receives a 3-digit industry within firm random effect that is two standard deviations above zero, an establishment that receives a random establishment effect of just one standard deviation below zero would have a tendency to contract. Note further that this analysis is not relying at all on residual variance, which would only lend further credence to this argument.

This last point on not relying on residual variance highlights one benefit of using job-level data to analyze employment growth at the firm or establishment level. Some portion of the variance of the residual term in Table 7 probably captures job-cell level shocks that have nothing to do with establishment productivity. An employee might move to a new state or drop out of the labor force unexpectedly even if the establishment's manager had no intention of reducing employment. Employment fluctuations due to these job-cell level shocks only affect our residual (job cell) variance, but do not affect the other variances in Table 7.

Suppose now that we only observed employment at the establishment level, as is common in the literature. We could estimate models with random firm effects, random 3-digit industry within firm effects, and random establishment effects, but our estimated variance of random establishment effects would incorporate job-cell level shocks in addition to the establishment-wide shocks. In this sense, our estimated variance of random establishment effects in Table 7 has a cleaner interpretation than would an estimated variance of a random establishment effect from data set with only establishment (rather than job cell) employment.

To illustrate this point empirically, we estimate a model of employment growth at the establishment level in Table 8. That is, our dependent variable is the percent change in total establishment employment, including jobs that were not specifically sampled in the NCS. Note that our estimated variances of random firm effects and random 3-digit industry within firm effects are similar to those in Table 7. The variance of the random establishment effect (the residual) is, as hypothesized, larger than the variance of the random establishment effect in Table 7 (more than twice as large). We therefore find that more than half of the establishment-level heterogeneity found in establishment-level employment changes comes from job-cell specific shocks. Using occupation-level data in Table 6, we are able to separate out these job-cell specific shocks, which arguably are less related to productivity than are establishment-wide shocks.

7. Conclusions

Diversified firms have establishments in different locales, with different occupational mixes, which operate in different industries. We use a unique data set that links labor-market information across establishments and business lines for these diversified firms to investigate, for the first time in the literature, the degree to which labor markets appear uniform throughout these diversified firms. We find the following:

1. Industries that employ high-wage occupations tend not to be linked under the same firm with industries that employ low-wage occupations.

2. Industries that pay high-wages (after controlling for occupational distributions and other covariates) tend not to be linked under the same firm with industries that pay low-wages.

3. Controlling for industry and occupation effects, wage levels are correlated across establishments and across major industries within diversified firms.

4. Wage changes are essentially uncorrelated across establishments within a firm.

5. Job-level employment changes are uncorrelated across 3-digit industries within a firm.

6. Job-level employment changes are correlated across establishments within a 3-digit industry within a firm, but establishment-specific shocks are much more important determinants of job-level employment changes.

References

Abowd, John M. and Francis Kramarz, 1999, "The Analysis of Labor Markets Using Matched Employer-Employee Data" in *Handbook of Labor Economics*, v3b, edited by Orley Ashenfelter and David Card, (Elsevier, Amsterdam).

Abowd, John M. and Francis Kramarz, 2000, "Inter-industry and Firm-size Wage Differentials: New Evidence from Linked Employer-Employee Data," mimeo, Cornell University

Abowd, John M., Francis Kramarz, and David N. Margolis, 1999, "High Wage Workers and High Wage Firms," *Econometrica*, v67, n2, 251-333.

Berger, Philip G. and Eli Ofek, 1995, "Diversification's Effect on Firm Value," *Journal of Financial Economics*, v37, n1, 39-65.

Bronars, Stephen G. and Melissa Famulari, 1997, "Wage, Tenure, and Wage Growth Variation Within and Across Establishments," *Journal Of Labor Economics*, v15, n2, 285-317.

Brown, Charles, and James Medoff, 1989, "The Employer Size-Wage Effect," *Journal of Political Economy*, v97, n5, 1027-1059.

Chevalier, Judith A., 2000, "What Do We Know About Cross-Subsidization? Evidence from the Investment Policies of Merging Firms," mimeo, University of Chicago.

Corporate Affiliations Plus, 1998 and 2000, Software purchased from the National Register Publishing Company covering the winter 1997-1998 and spring 2000 periods respectively.

Davis, Steven J. and John C. Haltiwanger, 1990, "Gross Job Creation and Destruction: Microeconomic Evidence and Macroeconomic Implications." *NBER Macroeconomics Annual*, 123-168.

Davis, Steven J. and John C. Haltiwanger, 1992. "Gross Job Creation, Gross Job Destruction, and Employment Reallocation." *Quarterly Journal of Economics*, v107, n3, 819-863.

Davis, Steven J. and John C. Haltiwanger, 1999, "Gross Job Flows," in *Handbook of Labor Economics*, v3b, edited by Orley Ashenfelter and David Card, (Elsevier, Amsterdam).

Groshen, Erica L., 1991, "Sources of Intra-Industry Wage Dispersion: How Much Do Employers Matter?" *Quarterly Journal of Economics*, v106, n3, 869-884.

Kremer, Michael, 1993, "The O-Ring Theory of Economic Development," *Quarterly Journal of Economics*, v108, n3, 551-575.

Lamont, Owen, 1997, "Cash Flow and Investment: Evidence from Internal Capital Markets," *Journal of Finance*, v52, n1, 83-109.

McGahan, Anita M. and Michael E. Porter, 1999, "The Persistence of Shocks to Profitability," *Review of Economics and Statistics*, v81, n1, 143-153.

Rumelt, Richard P., 1991, "How Much Does Industry Matter?" *Strategic Management Journal*, v 12, n3, 167-185.

Schmalensee, Richard, 1985, "Do Markets Differ Much?" *American Economic Review*, v75, n3, 341-351.

Searle, Shayle R., George Casella, and Charles E. McCulloch, 1992, *Variance Components*, (Wiley, New York).

Troske, Kenneth R., 1999, "Evidence on the Employer Size-Wage Premium from Worker-Establishment Matched Data," *Review of Economics and Statistics*, v81, n1, 15-26.

U.S. Department of Labor, Bureau of Labor Statistics Bulletin 2490, *Handbook of Methods*, April 1997, Washington, DC.

Table 1

Partial List of General Electric's Industries

- SIC=2821: plastics material and synthetic resins

- SIC=2865: cyclic organic crudes and intermediates

- SIC=3291: abrasive products

- SIC=3641: electric lamp bulbs and tubes

- SIC=3724: aircraft engines and engine parts

- SIC=3845: electromedical and electrotherapeutic apparatus

- SIC=4581: airports, flying fields, and airport terminal services

- SIC=4833: television broadcasting stations

- SIC=6159: miscellaneous business credit institutions

- SIC=6311: life insurance

- SIC=7371: computer programming services

- SIC=7515: passenger car leasing

Data are taken from Corporate Affiliations Plus (Spring 2000 edition). Data for this table are not taken from BLS sources. We make no claims about which components of General Electric, if any, appear in our sample.

Table 2
Sample Statistics

	Number	
Occupation-Establishment Cells	34,792	
Establishments	4,320	
Firms	1,020	
with multiple 3 digit industries	457	
with multiple major industries	258	

	Average	Standard Deviation
Average Log Wage, 1997-1998	2.652	0.579
Log Wage Growth, 1997-1998	0.022	0.096

Comparison of Multi-Establishment Panel to 1997 NCS Cross-Section

1997 values for:	Multi-Establishment Panel	1997 NCS
log wage	2.641	2.591
union coverage indicator	0.225	0.145
establishment employment	1,342.7	899.9
Occupation Distributions		
Professional	12.5	14.2
Technical	4.9	5.7
Executive	10.3	10.8
Sales	11.9	7.7
Clerical	18.4	19.5
Production, Craft	10.3	9.0
Operators, Assemblers	8.8	8.8
Transport, Material Moving	3.6	3.2
Handlers, Laborers	8.8	7.3
Service	10.7	13.9
Industry Distributions		
Mining	1.3	1.1
Construction	0.6	2.4
Nondurables Manufacturing	11.5	10.1
Durables Manufacturing	21.7	17.1
Transport, Communications, Utilities	9.8	6.2
Wholesale Trade	3.4	4.0
Retail Trade	22.4	14.2
FIRE	6.1	6.7
Services	23.3	38.3

Table 3

**Wage Level, Wage-Change, and Employment-Change Models
with Random Occupation, Industry, and Establishment Effects**

random effect		Log Wage Change		Log Wage		Employment Growth	
	variance	std error	variance	std error	variance	std error
occupation	0.00001	0.00001	0.144	0.011	0.000	0.000
industry	0.00003	0.00001	0.037	0.004	0.001	0.000
establishment	0.00091	0.00004	0.020	0.001	0.025	0.001
residual	0.00692	0.00006	0.051	0.000	0.159	0.001

Models are estimated using restricted maximum likelihood, and include fixed effects for union status, month of observation, and state. The models use 3 digit Census codes for occupations and 3 digit SIC codes for industry. Log Wage Change is the change in the Log Wage for the job cell from 1997-98. Log Wage is the average of Log Wages in 1997 and 1998. Employment Growth is the change in job-cell employment from 1997-98, divided by average employment in 1997 and 1998.

Table 4
Baseline Wage Models

random effect	Log Wage Growth		Log Wage	
	variance	std error	variance	std error
firm	0.0000	0.00005	0.0045	0.0013
firm*major industry	0.0000	NA	0.0058	0.0019
firm*3 digit industry	0.0001	0.00006	0.0049	0.0014
establishment	0.0007	0.00004	0.0089	0.0005
residual	0.0069	0.00006	0.0506	0.0004

Decomposing the within-Establishment Wage Correlation (Total Correlation = 0.32)

	Time-Varying Effects		Permanent Effects	
	variance	percent of correlation	variance	percent of correlation
firm	0.0000	0.0%	0.0045	18.5%
firm*major industry	0.0000	0.0%	0.0058	23.8%
firm*3 digit industry	0.0001	0.2%	0.0049	20.0%
establishment	0.0004	1.5%	0.0087	35.8%
residual	0.0034		0.0489	
total	0.0039	1.8%	0.0728	98.2%

Correlations across Job Cells

	wage levels	wage changes
same establishment; different job	0.32	0.11
same firm & 3 digit industry; different establishment	0.20	0.01
same firm & major industry; different 3 digit industry	0.13	0.00
same firm; different major industry	0.06	0.00

Models are estimated using restricted maximum likelihood, and include fixed effects for union status, month of observation, state, 3-digit industry, and 3-digit Census occupation code. In the wage-change model, the estimated variance of the random effect for major industry within firm is zero (the boundary). All other estimates and standard errors in the wage-change model impose that the major industry within firm coefficient is zero with certainty. All correlations are of the components of log wages (or changes in log wages) that are not explained by the fixed effects. The wage levels correlations in the final panel assume wage draws from the same year.

Table 5
Wage Models Including Establishment Size Controls

random effect	Log Wage Growth		Log Wage	
	variance	std error	variance	std error
firm	0.0000	0.0001	0.0012	0.001
firm*major industry	0.0000	0.0002	0.0072	0.002
firm*3 digit industry	0.0001	0.0002	0.0048	0.001
establishment	0.0007	0.0000	0.0085	0.000
residual	0.0069	0.0001	0.0506	0.000

Decomposing the within-Establishment Wage Correlation (Total Correlation = 0.30)

	Time-Varying Effects		Permanent Effects	
	variance	percent of correlation	variance	percent of correlation
firm	0.0000	0.0%	0.0012	5.4%
firm*major industry	0.0000	0.0%	0.0072	32.9%
firm*3 digit industry	0.0000	0.2%	0.0048	21.7%
establishment	0.0004	1.7%	0.0083	37.9%
residual	0.0034		0.0489	
total	0.0039	2.0%	0.0705	98.0%

Correlations across Job Cells

	wage levels	wage changes
same establishment; different job	0.30	0.11
same firm & 3 digit industry; different establishment	0.18	0.01
same firm & major industry; different 3 digit industry	0.11	0.00
same firm; different major industry	0.02	0.00

Models are estimated using restricted maximum likelihood, and include fixed effects for union status, month of observation, state, 3-digit industry, and 3-digit Census occupation code. Additional fixed effects include the log of the number of employees in the establishment, in the firm and 3-digit industry, in the firm and major industry, and in the entire firm. All correlations are of the components of log wages (or changes in log wages) that are not explained by the fixed effects. The wage levels correlations in the final panel assume wage draws from the same year.

Table 6
Wage Models, Non-union Sample

random effect	Log Wage Growth		Log Wage	
	variance	std error	variance	std error
firm	0.0000	0.0000	0.0026	0.0014
firm*major industry	0.0000	NA	0.0068	0.0022
firm*3 digit industry	0.0001	0.0001	0.0043	0.0016
establishment	0.0009	0.0001	0.0094	0.0006
residual	0.0077	0.0001	0.0518	0.0005

Decomposing the within-Establishment Wage Correlation (Total Correlation = 0.30)

	Time-Varying Effects		Permanent Effects	
	variance	percent of correlation	variance	percent of correlation
firm	0.0000	0.0%	0.0026	11.3%
firm*major industry	0.0000	0.0%	0.0068	29.0%
firm*3 digit industry	0.0001	0.2%	0.0042	18.2%
establishment	0.0004	1.8%	0.0092	39.4%
residual	0.0039		0.0498	
total	0.0043	2.1%	0.0727	97.9%

Correlations across Job Cells

	wage levels	wage changes
same establishment; different job	0.30	0.11
same firm & 3 digit industry; different establishment	0.18	0.01
same firm & major industry; different 3 digit industry	0.12	0.00
same firm; different major industry	0.03	0.00

Models are estimated using restricted maximum likelihood, and include fixed effects for union status, month of observation, state, 3-digit industry, and 3-digit Census occupation code. Additional fixed effects include the log of the number of employees in the establishment, in the firm and 3-digit industry, in the firm and major industry, and in the entire firm. All correlations are of the components of log wages (or changes in log wages) that are not explained by the fixed effects. The wage levels correlations in the final panel assume wage draws from the same year.

Table 7
Employment-Change Model with Random Firm, Random Firm within 3-Digit Industry, and Random Establishment Effects

Dependent Variable: Percentage Change in Employment for the Job Cell

random effect	variance	std error	percent of correlation
firm	0.0008	0.0011	3.1%
firm*3 digit industry	0.0043	0.0014	17.1%
establishment	0.0201	0.0011	79.8%
residual	0.1589	0.0013	

Employment-Change Correlations across Job Cells

same establishment	0.14
same firm & 3 digit industry; different establishments	0.03
same firm; different establishments & 3 digit industry	0.00

Model is estimated using restricted maximum likelihood, and includes fixed effects for union status, month of observation, state, 3-digit industry, and 3-digit Census occupation code. All correlations are of the components of employment changes that are not explained by the fixed effects.

Table 8
Employment-Change Model using Establishment Data with Random Firm and Random Firm within 3-Digit Industry Effects

Dependent Variable: Percentage Change in Employment for the Establishment

random effect	variance	std error	percent of correlation
firm	0.0008	0.0011	14.7%
firm*3 digit industry	0.0046	0.0014	85.3%
establishment	0.0451	0.0012	

Employment-Change Correlations across Establishments

same firm and same 3-digit industry	0.11
same firm but different 3-digit industries	0.02

Model is estimated using restricted maximum likelihood, and includes fixed effects for month of observation, state, and 3-digit industry. All correlations are of the components of employment changes that are not explained by the fixed effects.

Figure 1:
Stylized Structure of a Large Multi-Industry Firm

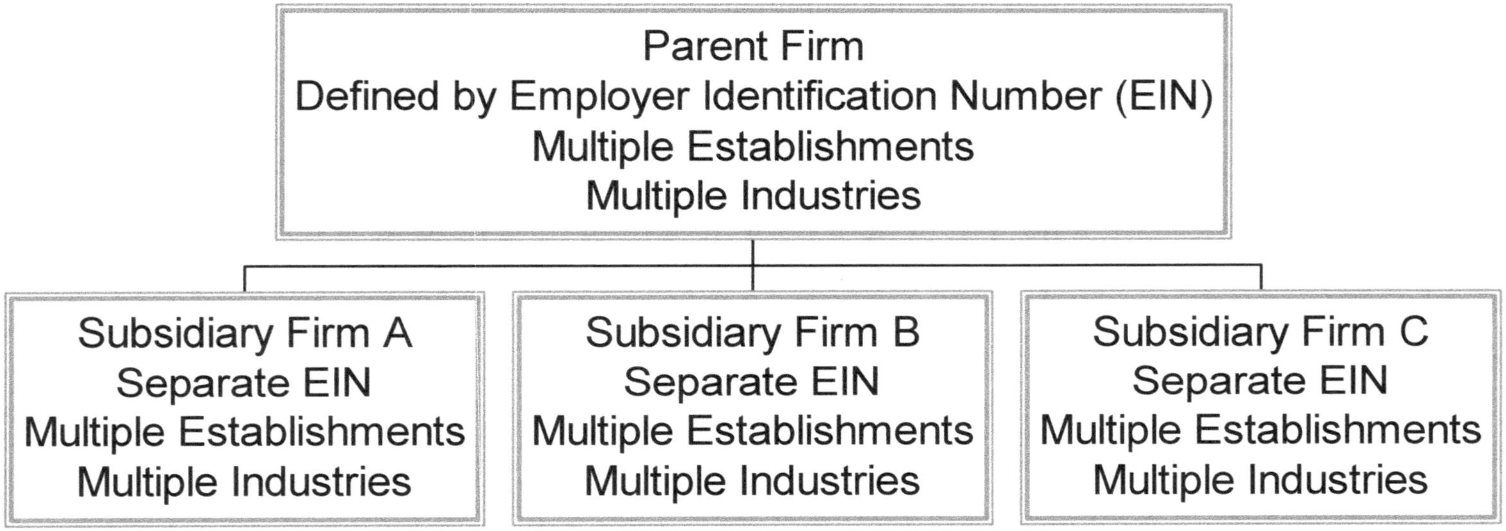

Parent Firm
Defined by Employer Identification Number (EIN)
Multiple Establishments
Multiple Industries

Subsidiary Firm A
Separate EIN
Multiple Establishments
Multiple Industries

Subsidiary Firm B
Separate EIN
Multiple Establishments
Multiple Industries

Subsidiary Firm C
Separate EIN
Multiple Establishments
Multiple Industries

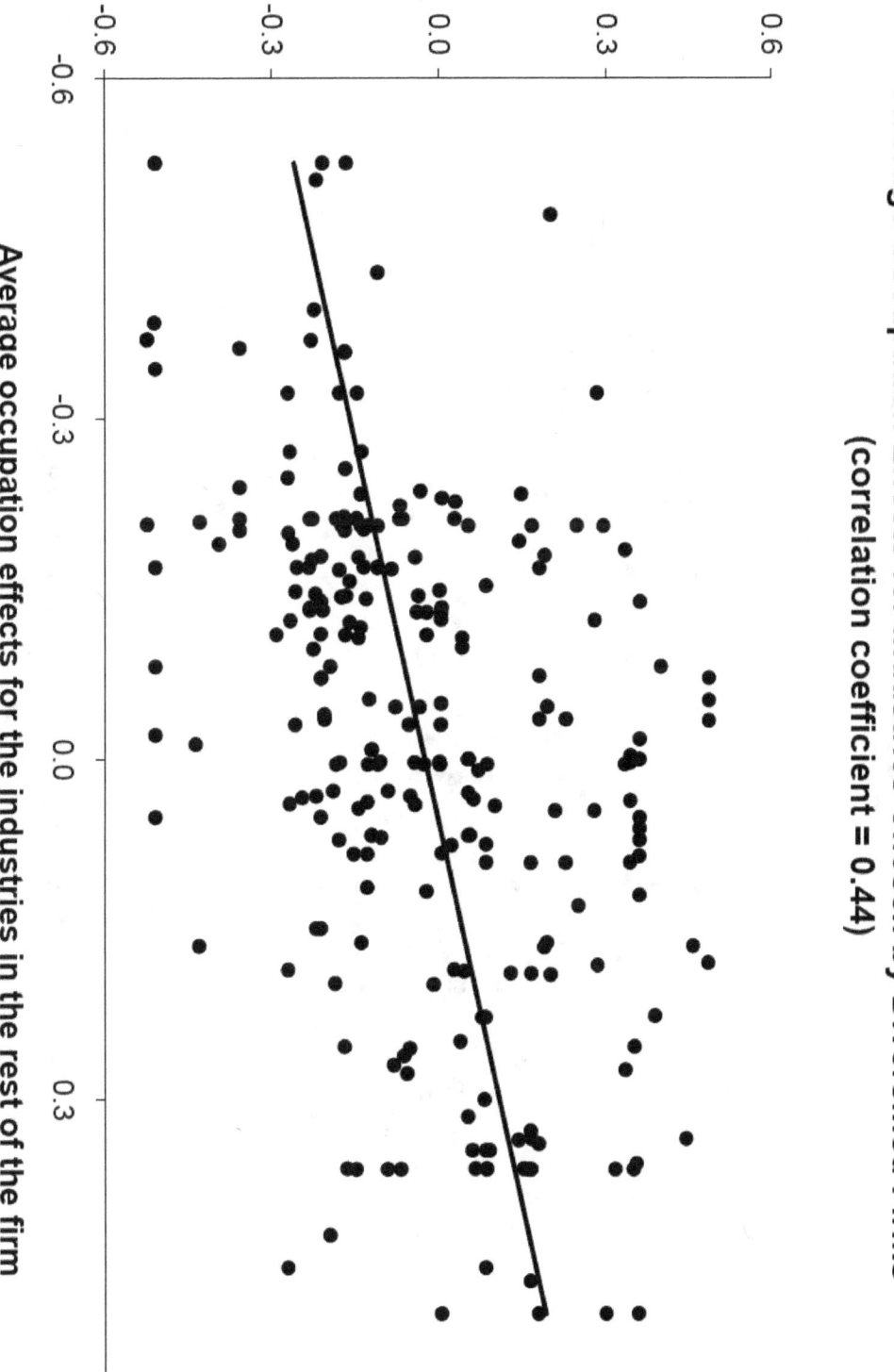

Figure 2:
Average Occupation Effects for Industries Chosen by Diversified Firms
(correlation coefficient = 0.44)

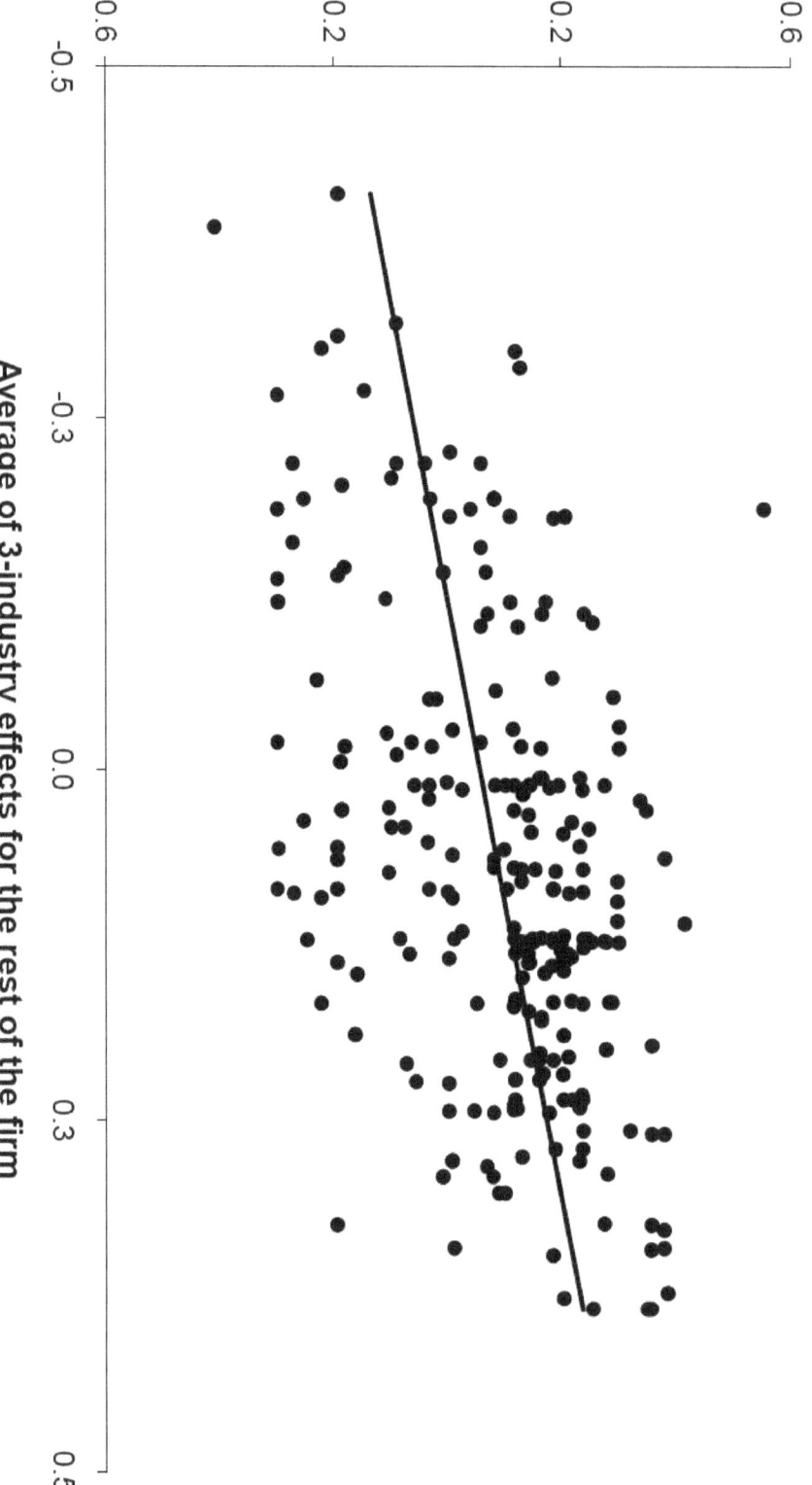

Figure 3:
Average Industry Effects for Diversified Firms
(correlation coefficient = 0.44)